Improving the Care of People in Substance Misuse Services: Clinical Audit Project Examples

Kirsty MacLean Steel and Claire Palmer

Published by Gaskell
London

WM
270
MAC

British Library Cataloguing-in-Publication Data
A catalogue record for this book is available from
the British Library.
ISBN 1-901242-46-3

29704

Printed by Henry Ling Limited, Dorchester, Dorset.

Improving the Care of People in Substance Misuse Services: Clinical Audit Project Examples

Contents

The clinical audit projects

Assessment

Clinical care

Organisational/management processes

User satisfaction and outcomes

Foreword

The Oxford English Dictionary defines 'audit' as "an official examination of accounts" or "a systematic review", from the Latin *auditus*, meaning 'hearing'. The contributors to this volume have drawn from all parts of this definition. They are themselves working across the country, across disciplines and with a wide range of substances. They have provided some systematic accounts of many important areas for practitioners who are tackling substance problems among, and together with, their client groups. They all pay particular attention to 'auditus'. The contributors insist that we listen to user satisfaction, and to their dissatisfaction. A considerable number are satisfied with the services they receive. A significant proportion of the audit presentations are focused on organisational and management processes: speedy assessment and recording of information, initiation of treatment, monitoring and reviewing, as well as communications with other professionals and agencies about patients.

Appropriateness and success of out-patient and in-patient detoxification reverberates throughout, with high rates of completion of out-patient detoxification from alcohol reported. The contributors recommend that evaluation of different treatment settings for different periods of time is an important aspect in the review of these procedures.

The opportunity to facilitate further improvements in health, e.g. hepatitis B and C testing and vaccination, are on the agenda of several services. The auditors analyse the administration of old and new additional prescription drugs (methadone or acamprosate respectively), and also that of additional medication, such as benzodiazepines. Concerns about the identification, recording and effects on staff and service users of clients' deaths from any cause, including methadone related deaths, are raised. One of the dissatisfactions are those anxieties relating to case closure in this context.

The findings indicate that interagency liaison is essential to mobilise the range of resources required to further improve services. The need for effective working relationships with accident and emergency units and psychiatric liaison services, especially in cases of deliberate self-harm, was highlighted.

It is well worth hearing what the contributors have to say, to take account of the lessons that they learned from their experiences, and to attempt to remedy the causes of frustrations and distress, while also acknowledging achievements.

Ilana B. Crome
Chair, Substance Misuse Faculty
Royal College of Psychiatrists

Acknowledgements

We would like to thank the following people for their invaluable help: Ilana Crome and Ken Checkinski from the Royal College of Psychiatrists' Substance Misuse Faculty; Mrs Pat Gibbs from Leicestershire and Rutland Healthcare NHS Trust; and Victoria Thomas and Sam Coombs at the College Research Unit.

We are also indebted to the following people for their help and generosity in sharing their work with us:

J. Bearn, Wickham Park House, Bethlem Royal Hospital

Barry Blackstone, Community Drugs Service

Neena Buntwal, Wickham Park House, Bethlem Royal Hospital

Wendy Burgess, North East Lincolnshire NHS Trust

Chris Daly, Wentworth House

Kristin Dominy, Wickham Park House, Bethlem Royal Hospital

Colin Drummond, St George's Hospital Medical School

Richard Elliott, South West Drug Services Audit Project

Exeter & District Community Health Service NHS Trust, Drugs and Alcohol Resource Team (DART)

T. J. Flanigan, Cheltenham Drug Team

Elaine Hadwen, Oxleas NHS Trust

Hastings Drug Dependency Unit

Angela Kerr, Dundonald Health Centre

Steve Owen, North Sefton and West Lancashire NHS Trust

Sally Porter, St George's Hospital Medical School

Andrew D. T. Robinson, Grampian Healthcare NHS Trust

Daphne Rumball, The Bure Centre

Robert Scott, Glasgow Drug Problem Service

John Sharpley, Defence Services Psychiatric Centre

Sally Spurrell, Royal Free Drug Services

Caroline Ward, Thames Gateway NHS Trust

Ruth White, Worcestershire Community Healthcare

Hazel Wright, Community Drugs Service

Introduction

Background: substance misuse

The recording of alcohol and drug problems in the UK is not currently comprehensive, with drug misuse surveys generally only being carried out on a regional basis. There are alcohol surveys that cover Great Britain, however, these may not be representative of all heavy drinkers because of sampling problems (e.g. surveying private households only). They can be useful for observing changing trends though.

4.7% of adults in the UK are alcohol dependent and 2.2% are dependent on drugs. Men are three times more likely to have alcohol problems than women (Meltzer *et al*, 1995). Single people are more likely to drink over the recommended limits than those who are married, and particularly those with dependent children. Among women, socio-economic factors seem to affect the pattern of alcohol dependence. Women in professional households are almost twice as likely as those in semi-skilled or unskilled households to drink more than the recommended limits. The same can be seen for those who work full-time compared with those who work part-time or do not work at all. In fact, as income increases the alcohol consumption of women increases. This pattern is not found in men (OPCS, 1996).

This latter pattern is very different to that found in drug misuse. Drug problems are seen more in areas of low economic activity, high unemployment and where there is a lack of opportunities for young people (Scottish Drugs Forum All-Party Policy Working Group, 1999). The Regional Drug Misuse Databases collect information on drug users presenting to drug misuse agencies in England. In the most recent report, covering the period September 1997 to March 1998, it was noted that the number of people presenting to services had increased by 9% from the previous month. As with alcohol dependency, men were three times more likely than women to have drug problems. The age breakdown showed that 33% of those presenting were aged 30 or over, 53% were 20–29 and 14% were under 20. 42% of users were recorded as misusing one drug, 28% as misusing two drugs and 30% as misusing three or more. 57% reported heroin as the main drug of use, 12% reported methadone and 9% reported amphetamines (Department of Health (DoH), 1999).

50% of drug users presenting to services were reported by statutory community based drug services, 29% by non-statutory community-based drug services, 6% by NHS funded groups and 7% by out-patient drug dependency units (DoH, 1999).

Background: clinical audit

In recent years, clinical audit has become an important part of all health services. The DoH Working Paper *Medical Audit* (1990) outlined the requirement for all doctors to participate in audit and throughout the 1990s this expectation expanded to include

Research
evidence

Patients'/
carers'
views

Clinical
experience

Re-audit to ensure
that changes:
(a) have been made
and
(b) have led to
improvement

Set explicit
standards

Implement
change

Measure
current
practice
against the
standards

Data
collection

Action
planning

Identify areas
where clinical
practice can be
improved

Data analysis/
results

Feedback
and group
discussion

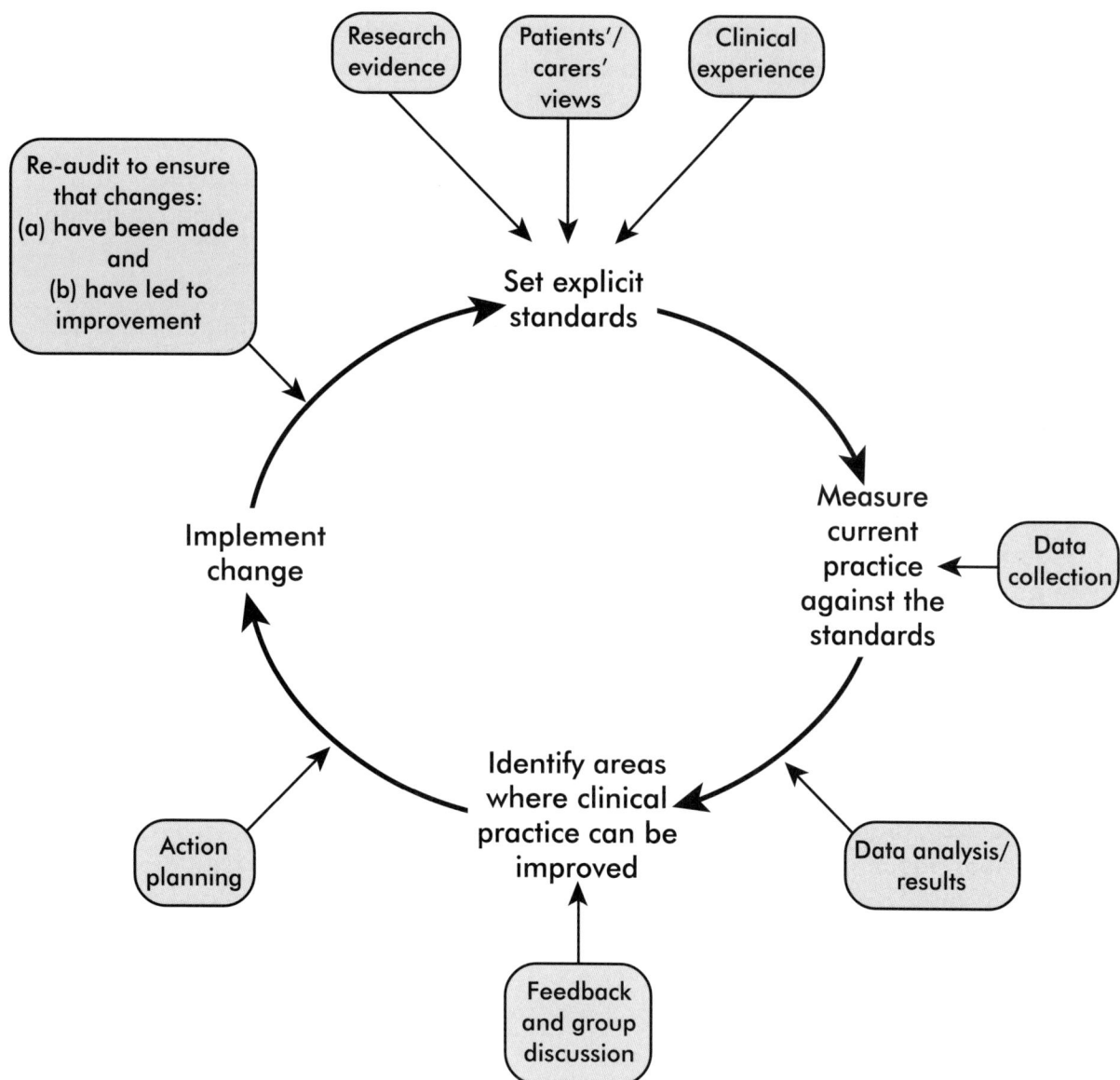

Fig. 1   The clinical audit cycle

clinicians of all professions. In 1997, the launch of the White Paper, *The New NHS: Modern, Dependable* (DoH, 1997), placed clinical audit as a core component of the new policy of clinical governance. Clinical governance imposes a new responsibility of quality onto NHS trusts, making the accountability and management of the quality of clinical care equally important as financial accountability and management. Lugon & Secker-Walker (1999) argue that:

"it follows that if quality standards are the central means of improving services, then the mechanism for monitoring and ensuring these are delivered will undoubtedly be clinical audit." (Lugon & Secker-Walker, 1999, p. 61)

Clinicians should see a renewed emphasis on and priority for clinical audit within their trusts. The practical implications of this should include management support for the implementation of changes identified through audit, support from training departments for training in clinical audit methods and support from managers in helping clinicians to identify time and priorities for clinical audit. Clinical audit is a useful and practical method of ascertaining whether services provided are effective, efficient and of a high quality. It is used to review practice by systematically monitoring whether clinical care meets pre-agreed standards, identifying areas in which change is needed and outlining an action plan for improvement.

As this book will demonstrate, many aspects of care and treatment (from admission to discharge and beyond) are amenable to clinical audit. Clinical audit should not be a difficult or daunting prospect – small projects focusing on narrow areas of practice are often as worthwhile as more complex ones. Clinical audit is a multi-disciplinary activity, with all staff whose practice is included in the audit being involved from the beginning of the project.

There are several points which are crucial to carrying out successful clinical audit:
- careful planning;
- setting clear and measurable standards;
- setting standards on the basis of evidence where possible;
- taking a multi-disciplinary approach;
- if questionnaires are to be used, ensuring the responses can be clearly interpreted and analysed;
- being clear about methods of analysis when planning a project; and
- avoiding complicated projects – simple ones usually achieve the most and are easiest to carry out.

The aim of the book

This book was produced by the Clinical Governance Support Service at the Royal College of Psychiatrists' Research Unit. It is intended to support people in substance misuse services who are undertaking, or planning to undertake, clinical audit projects, by:
- providing ideas for project topics;
- providing ideas for project methods;
- providing examples of standards from other services which they can use locally;
- facilitating benchmarking against other services' standards; and
- providing contact details of others who have undertaken clinical audit projects in substance misuse services.

The contents of the book

The book contains 28 clinical audit projects, all of which have been carried out in practice, with some still in progress. The projects have been divided into topic areas and formatted into structured abstracts for ease of use.

It is hoped that the information about the clinical audit projects included in this Pack is sufficient to help anyone undertaking an audit to begin to design their own project.

All the projects in this book were submitted by either the Clinical Audit Lead or the Clinical Audit Department from a variety of NHS trusts. We were overwhelmed by the enthusiasm and support of these individuals and groups. We hope that those reading the book will be inspired by the great range of projects.

Themes arising from the projects

Some useful points were raised by the contributors to this publication that are worth considering outside of the context of any particular clinical audit project:

- Involve team members at all levels as much as possible and as early as possible.
- Make sure the data being audited are available.
- Set reasonable standards after consultation with the whole team.
- Be prepared for a lot of work.
- Don't take on too much.
- Ensure good liaison between all departments.
- Keep things simple.

Key to reading the clinical audit project reports

Background | Why the audit was considered important.

Aim | The aims and objectives of the project.

Standards | Measurable standards against which practice was compared.

Evidence | Evidence on which the standards were based.

Staff involved | The staff involved in the clinical audit project.

Sample | The patients, clients, etc. involved in the project.

Data collection | How the data were collected.

Data analysis | What type of analysis the data were subjected to.

Key findings | Findings relating to the standards.

Feedback | Who the findings were fed back to and in what form.

Change | Suggestions for changes in practice arising from the findings. Also any significant things which either helped or prevented change from being implemented.

Re-audit | Plans for re-audit.

Resources | The amount of staff time taken to complete the audit cycle and other costs or resources needed.

Notes | Problems encountered in undertaking the clinical audit project, aspects that the contributors would change if repeating the project and advice for anyone attempting to conduct a similar audit.

Contact | Details of the person to whom further enquiries about the specific project example should be directed.

Shading draws attention to stages of the clinical audit cycle which are crucial and which are often omitted.

This book contains examples of 'real-life' clinical audit projects. The projects demonstrate the range of audit topics and methods undertaken in substance misuse services, and the information has been willingly volunteered by people working within these services. Some of the examples do not contain information under all the above headings.

The projects in this book are not intended to be recommended as gold standard audit projects.

Important note

The projects described in this book have been submitted to the Royal College of Psychiatrists' Research Unit by mental health service staff. Inclusion in this book does not indicate endorsement by the Research Unit, and the College takes no responsibility for the quality of the projects reported herein. All questions concerning specific projects should be directed to the submitting trust.

The clinical audit projects

Assessment

Aim	To improve organisational processes.

Standards

1 All assessments must be carried out by a staff member familiar with the agency's procedures.
2 The assessments must include a record of:
- the name, gender and date of birth of the client;
- baseline data against which changes can be measured including data on: illicit drug use; prescribed drug use; injecting practice, if any; physical health; psychological health; legal situation; domiciliary situation; employment/training/childcare situation; clients' perceptions of problem(s), need(s) and primary goals; worker's perceptions of problem(s) and need(s);
- a check to ensure confidentiality policy and implications are explained;
- a check to ensure that, where possible, the client is offered a choice of gender of caseworker;
- a check to ensure that safer sex issues are raised and a note if further discussion/information is needed, and if not, why not;
- the name and address of general practitioner (GP)/probation officer/ social worker/solicitor as appropriate;
- a check to ensure that the client has access to a GP or another source of primary health care with which they are satisfied;
- a record of action taken if the answer to the previous point is negative;
- a record of clients' consent for the release of information where appropriate;
- the completion of a Regional Drug Misuse Database form.
- details of action taken, or not, as a result of the assessment must be recorded (but this does not have to be on the assessment form itself).

Sample

6 clients assessed in 12 months.

Key findings

All standards met except:
- a check to ensure that the client has access to a GP or another source of primary health care with which they are satisfied – *standard partially met as there is no section of the assessment for recording client satisfaction with their primary healthcare;* and
- a record of action taken if the answer to the previous point is negative – *standard not met.*

Change

Assessment documentation has been modified to include a place to record whether a client has access to a GP or another source of primary health care with which they are satisfied and any action taken if the answer to this is negative.

Contact

David Axon, Nurse/Manager of Drugs and Alcohol Resource Team (DART), Exeter & District Community Health Service NHS Trust, Wonford House Hospital, Dryden Road, Wonford, Exeter, EX2 5AF. Tel: 01392 208210; fax: 01392 208217.

Assessment of patients presenting for treatment

Background

For the last three years an audit has been undertaken of the quality of new patient assessments. Through review of past audit, systems have been developed to ensure that quality of assessment is maintained with particular respect to ensuring liaison with GPs, health screening and compliance with requirements of the Substance Misuse Database and Home Office Notification procedures.

Aim

To evaluate the standard of assessment procedures at a drug dependency unit.

Standards

1 Referral letters from GPs must be acknowledged on receipt.
2 Letters informing GPs of outcome of assessment must be sent within 5 working days.
3 The Substance Use Database recording form and Home Office notification must be completed.
4 Patients must be offered health screening to include hepatitis testing and human immunodeficiency virus (HIV) counselling.

Evidence

Local quality standards.

Staff involved

All members of the multi-disciplinary team.

Sample

12 patients randomly selected from a 12-month period.

Data collection

From case notes.

Data analysis

Simple frequencies were calculated.

Key findings

- 100% of referral letters from GPs were acknowledged on receipt.
- 90% of letters informing GPs of outcome of assessment were sent within 5 working days. 2 patients did not have GPs.
- The Substance Use Database recording form and Home Office notification were completed in 100% of cases.
- 100% of patients were tested for hepatitis and 60% received HIV counselling.

Feedback

Results presented to the regular Clinical Audit Meeting. Findings were published in the Annual Audit Report.

Change

The low figure for HIV counselling was identified as a consequence of recent service reconfigurations. This had now been addressed.

Re-audit

12 months later.

Resources used

10 hours project co-ordinator and doctor.

Contact

Dr Sally Porter, Senior Lecturer, St George's Hospital Medical School, Department of Addictive Behaviour & Psychological Medicine, Cranmer Terrace, London, SW17 0RE. Tel: 0181 682 6931; fax: 0181 682 6937; email: sporter@sghms.ac.uk

Evaluation of home and hospital alcohol detoxification services

Aim	To ensure that each client entering the service receives detoxification in an appropriate setting – either social (home or out-patient) or medical (hospital).
Standards	1 All clients and carers must receive advice concerning: • provision of emergency contact telephone number • appropriate diet • obtaining and taking Vitamin B1 • stopping medication if resumption of alcohol intake occurs. 2 All clients must have been visited by a member of the substance misuse team at least once during the first 4 days and on completion of the detoxification. 3 Each client's GP must receive a letter detailing the client's previous drinking pattern and progress of the detoxification.
Evidence	Local consensus.
Staff involved	Registrar and member of Clinical Audit Department.
Sample	64 clients undergoing home detoxification and 54 clients undergoing hospital detoxification over a 3-month period.
Data collection	Case note review.
Data analysis	Descriptive statistics.
Key findings	• 11% of clients and carers received advice concerning provision of an emergency contact telephone number, appropriate diet, obtaining and taking Vitamin B1 and stopping medication if resumption of alcohol intake occurs. 9% received advice on 3 of these, 30% received advice on 2, 25% received advice on 1, and no advice was documented for 25%. • 89% of clients were visited by a member of the substance misuse team. Of those that completed four days of detoxification, 68% were visited daily for the first 4 days. • 42% of the home detoxification clients' and 65% of the residential group's GPs received a letter detailing the client's previous drinking pattern and progress of the detoxification. 5 clients were excluded as the GP had initiated the detoxification.
Feedback	Results were discussed with the Substance Misuse Team and with medical staff involved with hospital detoxifications.
Change	None recorded.
Re-audit	Currently underway.
Contact	John Sharpley, Defence Services Psychiatric Centre, DKH, Catterick Garrison, North Yorkshire, DL9 4DF. Tel: 01748 873167; fax: 01748 873142.

Care of long-term patients attending for protracted treatment programmes

Background	For the last 3 years, an audit has been undertaken of the quality of new patient assessments. Although all patients in continuing care are subject to regular review at follow-up appointments by individual keyworkers and doctors from the drug dependency unit and systematically by the multi-disciplinary team, a systematic audit of long-term patient care has not been presented.
Aim	To determine the quality of care provision in long-term care at a drug dependency service. Long-term care was defined as a treatment episode lasting for longer than 6 months.
Standards	1 All entries into case notes must be signed and dated. 2 Staff discipline must be identified. 3 The patient's name must be identified on each continuation sheet. 4 Standard departmental medical case histories must be typed. 5 At least 3 letters must be written to the patient's GP each year. 6 All patients must be offered hepatitis/HIV testing. 7 Whether the patient was informed of the results must be recorded. 8 All relevant patients must be offered a hepatitis B vaccination. 9 All relevant patients must be referred to a liver clinic. 10 Treatment must reflect the care plan.
Evidence	Local quality standards.
Staff involved	All members of the multi-disciplinary team.
Sample	A random sample of 20 long-term patients.
Data collection	From case notes.
Data analysis	Simple frequencies were calculated.
Key findings	• 96% of entries into case notes were signed and dated. • Staff discipline was identified in 70% of cases. • The patient's name was identified on each continuation sheet in 76% of cases. • Standard departmental medical case histories were typed in 94% of cases. • At least 3 letters were written to the patient's GP in 50% of cases. • 100% of patients were offered hepatitis/HIV testing. • 100% of patients were informed of the results and had this recorded. • 90% of relevant patients were offered a hepatitis B vaccination. • Treatment reflected the care plan in 85% of cases.
Feedback	Results presented to the regular clinical audit meeting. Findings were published in the Annual Clinical Audit Report.

| Change | • Staff were formally reminded of the requirement to sign, date and identify designation on all case notes entries. Keyworker to be responsible for ensuring that all pages in case notes are named and that case notes are in good condition. |
| | • The Team Coordinator is to develop protocols to ensure that keyworkers 'flag up' outstanding and ongoing tasks. A minimum standard for liaison with GPs has been agreed (at least 3 times a year for long-term patients). |

Re-audit   In 6 and 12 months.

Resources used Staff time for audit approximately 10 hours.

Contact   Dr Sally Porter, Senior Lecturer, St George's Hospital Medical School, Department of Addictive Behaviour & Psychological Medicine, Cranmer Terrace, London, SW17 0RE. Tel: 0181 682 6931; fax: 0181 682 6937; email: sporter@sghms.ac.uk

CLINICAL CARE

Client review

Background   Clients are reviewed during a team meeting at the Thursday prescribing clinic. Individual keyworkers are responsible for bringing clients' cases to review and recording the outcome in a review book.

Aim   To improve organisational processes.

Standards
1 Date of first review must be between 3 and 6 months from initial assessment.
2 Each subsequent review must be between 3 and 6 months from the last.
3 Reviews must be carried out by a staff member familiar with the agency's procedures.
4 Reviews must record changes in:
   • illicit drug use
   • prescribed drug use
   • physical health
   • psychological health
   • legal situation
   • domiciliary situation
   • employment/training/childcare situation
   • clients' perceptions of problem(s) and need(s)
   • worker's perceptions of problems(s) and need(s)
   • agreed goals
   • the name and address of GP/probation officer/social worker, if any.
5 Check to ensure any changes to confidentiality issues are explained.
6 Check to ensure the client has access to a GP or another source of primary health care with which they are satisfied.
7 Record of action taken if the answer to Standard 6 is negative.
8 Check to ensure that safer sex issues noted at assessment have been addressed, and if not, why not.
9 Date of next review recorded in notes.

Evidence   Review of clinical notes.

Staff involved   Team.

Sample   Records of 6 randomly selected clients.

Data collection   From records.

Key findings
• For standards 1 and 2, review dates could not be ascertained as the review book was not available for audit.
• 100% of reviews were carried out by qualified staff but it was not possible to ascertain if they were familiar with agency procedures.
• Only illicit drug use, prescribed drug use, physical health, psychological health, legal situation were documented in the case notes.
• Check to ensure any changes to confidentiality issues are explained – *standard not met*.
• Check to ensure the client has access to a GP or another source of primary health care with which they are satisfied – *client's access to a*

GP or another source of primary health care was recorded in all cases, but satisfaction was not.

- Record of action taken if the response to standard 6 is negative – *standard not met.*
- Check to ensure that safer sex issues noted at assessment have been addressed, and if not, why not – *standard not met.*
- Date of next review – *standard not met as there is now specific review documentation to record this.*

Feedback

Written report by auditors and verbal feedback.

Change

- A thorough review of the Client Review procedures was recommended.
- A method of gaining a quick overview of clients' progress was suggested.

Re-audit

In 12 months.

Contact

David Axon, Nurse/Manager of Drugs and Alcohol Resource Team (DART), Exeter & District Community Health Service NHS Trust, Wonford House Hospital, Dryden Road, Wonford, Exeter, EX2 5AF. Tel: 01392 208210; fax: 01392 208217.

CLINCIAL CARE

Hepatitis B vaccination

Aims	• To improve clinical processes, health outcomes and service user/carer satisfaction. • To highlight the area of project deficit.
Standards	1 All injecting clients must be actively encouraged to seek a hepatitis B vaccination. 2 Total number of injecting clients seen within time period must be recorded. 3 Total number of injecting clients with whom a hepatitis B vaccination was discussed must be recorded. 4 Details of clients with whom a hepatitis B vaccination was not discussed must be recorded, and reason(s) why not. 5 Clients' choices must be recorded. 6 Action taken by agency in support of clients' choices must be recorded.
Evidence	Audit project team discussed formulation of standards.
Staff involved	All Community Drug Service staff and peer auditors.
Sample	All injecting clients seen in time period.
Data analysis	Structured interview.
Key findings	In progress.
Re-audit	Annually.
Contact	Dr Barry Blackstone, Community Drugs Service, Danerel House, Danerel Close, Off Malden Road, Devonport, Plymouth, PL1 4JX. Tel: 01752 566670; fax: 01752 566676.

Hepatitis B vaccination programme

Background
: Hepatitis B is a serious, preventable disease that is transmitted parenterally and sexually. Immunisation is recommended in individuals who are at increase risk of hepatitis B because of their lifestyle, occupation or other factors. A hepatitis B vaccination programme was established at the Drug Dependency Unit, with routine collection of specific data relating to completion rates.

Aim
: To determine the completion rate and effectiveness of the hepatitis B vaccination programme.

Standards
: All individuals who commence vaccination programmes must complete the course (3 injections at 0 months, 1 month and 6 months).

Evidence
: National standards of good clinical practice – hepatitis B vaccination. DoH (1996) *Immunisation against Infectious Disease*. London: HMSO. Local quality standards.

Staff involved
: Programme Coordinator and doctor.

Sample
: Clients commencing programmes in August 1995–June 1996 (*n*=23).

Data collection
: Data collected from Hepatitis B Vaccination Programme monitoring forms.

Data analysis
: Simple frequencies were calculated.

Key findings
:
- 18 (78.3%) individuals who commenced vaccination programmes completed the course. 5 (21.7%) individuals defaulted.
- 100% of defaulters were written to.

Feedback
: Results were presented at the regular clinical audit meeting and published in the Annual Audit Report.

Change
: The programme was continued.

Resources used
: For each patient, a data collection form was completed at each attendance. Analysis of the data took approximately 3 hours.

Contact
: Dr Sally Porter, Senior Lecturer, St George's Hospital Medical School, Department of Addictive Behaviour & Psychological Medicine, Cranmer Terrace, London, SW17 0RE. Tel: 0181 682 6931; fax: 0181 682 6937; email: sporter@sghms.ac.uk

CLINICAL CARE

Hepatitis B and C testing and hepatitis B vaccination in the in-patient drug dependency unit

Background
: High-risk population for exposure to blood-borne viruses.
Hepatitis B vaccination is a good prophylactic measure.

Aims
: - To improve clinical processes, health outcomes and use of resources.
  - To assess current level of testing and vaccination.
  - To set standards for testing and vaccination.
  - To alter paperwork and process to facilitate standards.
  - Ensure good communication with GPs.

Standards
: 1 Establish hepatitis B & C status in 90% of admissions.
  2 Offer vaccine to 75% of hepatitis B-negative patients.
  3 For early leavers, inform GP of follow-up in 95% of cases.
  4 Inform GP of continuing care needs in 95% of cases.

Evidence
: Local consensus following initial 'benchmarking' of current practice.

Staff involved
: Ward doctors, administration staff and nursing staff.

Sample
: Initial audit - all discharges from the ward between 19 January 1998 and 24 February 1998 (54 patients)

Data collection
: From medical notes and discharge summaries.

Data analysis
: Descriptive statistics.

Key findings
: - Hepatitis B & C status achieved in 75.9%.
  - Vaccine given to 25%.
  - GPs informed in 95.5% of early leavers.
  - GPs informed of continuing needs in 98.1%.

Feedback
: Results communicated to quarterly Addictions Directorate Multi-Disciplinary Audit Meeting.

Change
: - Blood results to be actively followed up.
  - Change in routine documentation given to GPs.
  - Vaccines to be charted at weekly management rounds.
  - Nursing staff regularly checking vaccine prescriptions.
  - Discharge notification documentation was being reviewed at the same time. This helped to incorporate the audit suggestions and made it easier to re-audit the standards.

Re-audit
: Re-audit took place 1–31 May 1998. Intend to re-audit annually.

Resources used
: 6 hours for first audit and 2 hours for re-audit.

Notes
: For the initial audit, the poor design of the documentation made the data collection very difficult. After altering the documentation, the audit is a much simpler process and should be easy to repeat at regular intervals to help maintain standards.
  Advice: Keep the data collection as simple as possible. Set reasonable standards after consultation with the whole team.

Contact   Dr J. Bearn/Kristin Dominy, Wickham Park House, Bethlem Royal
                 Hospital, Monks Orchard Road, Beckenham, Kent, BR3 3BX. Tel: 0181
                 776 4114; fax: 0181 776 2026.

Outcomes of out-patient alcohol detoxification clinic

Background	First audit of a newly established nurse-led out-patient alcohol detoxification clinic.
Aim	To demonstrate efficacy or otherwise of service by examining effect on in-patient days for clients.
Standards	Individuals must show clear desire to stop drinking and there must be evidence of the risk of withdrawal symptoms.
Evidence	CRAG Working Group on Mental Illness (1994) *The Management of Alcohol Withdrawal and Delirium Tremens*. Lothian: CRAG.
Staff involved	1 E-grade nurse running the clinic. External evaluation by auditor.
Sample	32 patients who underwent out-patient detoxification in a 6-month period.
Data collection	From case notes.
Data analysis	Descriptive statistics.
Key findings	• 75% of clients successfully completed the out-patient detoxification programme. • 46.9% of clients had a Blood Alcohol Count of 0 when starting the programme. However these clients were no more successful at detoxifying than those with a positive count. • 21.9% of clients had had an admission to the out-patient programme during the previous 6 months. Of these, 71.4% had successfully completed the programme at that time. • 15.6% had evidence of previous delirium tremens, while 3.1% had evidence of epilepsy.
Change	Although no fits occurred, such patients were not to be detoxified in this setting.
Re-audit	To occur in a year.
Contact	Dr Andrew D. T. Robinson, Consultant Psychiatrist, Grampian Healthcare NHS Trust, Substance Misuse Service, Fulton Clinic, Royal Cornhill Hospital, Aberdeen. Tel: 01224 663131; fax: 01224 404975.

CLINICAL CARE

Self-harm and self-induced poisoning

Background   This project aimed to review the extent to which the Psychiatric Self-Harm Liaison Nurse is involved in the service. Maximising the use of this role will ensure that patients receive the best quality care.

Aims
- To follow patient from presentation in accident and emergency (A&E) to ward and follow-up post-discharge and ensure that standards were maintained.
- To improve clinical and organisational processes and use of resources.

Standards

A&E
1 Age and gender of patient and date and time patient presented to the A&E department must be recorded.
2 The type and quantity of substance must be documented. If not known, this must be documented.
3 Ingestion of alcohol must be documented.
4 The Poison Centre must be contacted and information and advice received must be documented. A copy of this must always remain with the A&E notes.
5 All patients presenting with self-harm discharged from the A&E department must have their notes photocopied and be referred to the Psychiatric Self-Harm Liaison Nurse.

Psychiatry
6 All patients admitted to the ward must be referred to the Psychiatric Self-Harm Liaison Nurse within 24 hours of admission.
7 All self harm patients discharged from A&E must be followed up with a visit or a letter within 4 days.
8 All patients' GPs must be informed.

Evidence   Royal College of Psychiatrists (1994) *The General Hospital Management of Adult Deliberate Self Harm*. London: Royal College of Psychiatrists.

Staff involved   A&E Consultant, staff nurses, Psychiatric Self-Harm Liaison Nurse, Audit Officer.

Sample   181 patients, representing a 3-month sample of presentations of self-harm.

Data collection   Retrospectively from notes.

Data analysis   Epidemiology Information analysis package.

Key findings   Audit still in progress.

Feedback   Presented to clinicians in general medicine, A&E and psychiatry and nursing staff during audit meetings.

Change   Audit still in progress.

Re-audit   6 months.

Resources used   Unknown.

Notes   Problems including a lack of documented times and alcohol taking.
               There were difficulties presenting findings to nursing staff in A&E. If doing
               this project again Parvolex set up would be included where necessary
               and the medical admission side of the process would be given greater
               emphasis.
               Advice: Ensure good liaison between all departments.

Contact   Wendy Burgess, Clinical Audit Department, c/o Diana Princess of Wales
               Hospital, North East Lincolnshire NHS Trust, Scartho Road, Grimsby,
               DN33 2BA. Tel: 01472 875406; fax: 01472 875670.

Case closures

Aims	• To monitor planned and unplanned case closures. • To improve organisational processes.
Standards	1 Reasons for case closures must be recorded. 2 A case list of all clients in regular contact must be available. 3 A policy document or set of practice guidelines must be available that clearly state: • under what circumstances a client's file must be closed; • within what time period a client's file must be closed; and • who must be informed of a case closure. 4 Records of case closures must be available by category and in accordance with the agency's policy and/or practice guidelines.
Evidence	South West Drug Audit Project standards.
Sample	6 randomly chosen files.
Key findings	• It was not noted whether reasons for case closures were recorded. • A case list of all clients in regular contact was available. • The new draft of the Case Closure Policy is detailed and comprehensive. • Records of case closures were available by category and in accordance with the agency's policy and/or practice guidelines.
Change	None.
Contact	David Axon, Nurse/Manager of Drugs and Alcohol Resource Team (DART), Exeter & District Community Health Service NHS Trust, Wonford House Hospital, Dryden Road, Wonford, Exeter, EX2 5AF. Tel: 01392 208210; fax: 01392 208217.

ORGANISATIONAL/MANAGEMENT PROCESSES

Deaths by cause

Background   Every 2 months, an audit is conducted on a single topic, with all participating agencies auditing the same topic simultaneously.

Aim   To learn if agencies are aware of client deaths and have systems in place to keep themselves informed of such deaths.

Standards   All agencies must be kept informed and have records of client deaths and cause of death.

Sample   20 agencies.

Data collection   Specially designed form.

Data analysis   Descriptive statistics.

Key findings
- 11 agencies (55%) fully met the standard.
- 7 (35%) partially met the standard.
- 2 (10%) did not meet the standard.

Change
- The DoH and the Coroner's Office should cooperate at a national level to cross-tabulate data from the Regional Drug Misuse Databases against national records of all deaths. Drug agencies could then be informed by the Department of Health if any of their clients or ex-clients have had their deaths recorded by the Coroner.
- Agencies should keep a register of case closures. The register should specify the reason for closure, including death, so that these figures could be readily accessed.
- Agencies should examine the effects of client deaths on both the agency as a whole and individual workers.
- Agencies should, where possible, keep records of persons referred for assessment or treatment who died before being seen.
- The effects of waiting times and discharges owing to changes in the level of service should be researched to assess their effect on mortality.
- Agencies may wish to keep a 'Remembrance Book' as a record of client and ex-client deaths.

Contact   Richard Elliott, Audit Coordinator, South West Drug Services Audit Project, Cedar House, Blackberry Hill Hospital, Bristol, BS16 2EW. Tel: 0117 958 6006; fax: 0117 958 6569; email: swdsap@bsds.demon.co.uk

Drug team service processes

Background	The county wide Substance Misuse Group convened at the Health Authority requested an audit of the structure of the service.
Aims	• To identify whether protocols are uniformly applied. • To ensure that new cases are allocated to correct routes through the system. • To improve organisational processes, service user/carer satisfaction and use of resources.

Standards	1 All patients identified as requiring medication prescriptions must be assessed by a clinical nurse specialist.
	2 All patients must have a clinic appointment with the clinical nurse specialist within 7 working days of receipt of the referral.
	3 Where assessment occurs, all the items detailed in the allocation criteria must be assessed.
	4 All patients must be allocated to the correct prescriber in accordance with the criteria detailed in the county-wide policy.
	5 All patients receiving methadone prescriptions must:
	  • satisfy the requirements of the methadone prescribing protocol;
	  • collect the methadone a minimum of 3 times a week during the first 2 weeks of the prescription;
	  • be observed swallowing the methadone on one occasion; and
	  • receive information about methadone.
	6 All cases under the care of the community drugs team for stabilisation must:
	  • be reviewed after 6 months; and
	  • have the outcomes recorded.
	7 In all cases where the patient is under the care of a prescribing GP and a clinical nurse specialist:
	  • the patient, GP and nurse must all be involved in devising a treatment plan;
	  • the patient must be reviewed by the nurse and GP in Month 2 of the programme; and
	  • the patient must be reviewed by the nurse and GP in Month 3 of the programme.
	8 In all cases where the patient is in the GP prescribing programme and Clinical Assistant Prescribing clinic he or she must:
	  • receive weekly visits during the first month of treatment;
	  • have a minimum of 2 random urinalysis drugs test in any 6-month period.

Evidence	County-wide treatment protocols.
Staff involved	2 nurses, drug teams and audit departments in 2 trusts.
Sample	Referrals to the drug teams.
Data collection	From case notes.
Key findings	None – in progress.
Feedback	The Mental Health Directorate.

Re-audit	To be decided on outcome.
Resources used	2 0.5 whole time equivalent nurses.
Contact	Mr T. J. Flanigan, Cheltenham Drug Team, Brownhill Centre, St Pauls, Cheltenham, Gloucester. Tel: 01242 272430.

Clinical audit in substance misuse services

ORGANISATIONAL/MANAGEMENT PROCESSES

Ethnicity of community alcohol team referrals

Background

It was found in a previous audit that the Community Alcohol Team (CAT) had a higher representation of clients from ethnic minorities than is reflected in the general population. Since that audit, data has been collected to examine trends and to gain a larger sample for comparison of ethnic minority subgroups.

Aim

To establish the ethnic composition of referrals to the Community Alcohol Team (CAT) in order to establish whether alcohol misusers from ethnic minority groups have equity of access to alcohol treatment services.

Standards

Ethnicity of clients must be recorded.

Evidence

Pathfinder Core Quality Standards (1995) 13.1. Pathfinder NHS Trust internal document. (NB Pathfinder NHS Trust is now South West London and St George's NHS Trust.)
DoH (1991) *The Patient's Charter*. London: HMSO.

Staff involved

All members of the team record patients' ethnicity at the point of first contact. Community psychiatric nurse collated data as part of a dissertation for the Diploma in Addictive Behaviour course, St George's Hospital Medical School, University of London. Data entered and analysed by CAT Administration Assistant.

Sample

Referrals to CAT in a 1-year period (*n*=381).

Data collection

Ethnicity is recorded in 1 of 9 categories (see 'Key findings') at the point of first contact by the assessing clinician using tick boxes on a pro forma Substance Use Database recording form.

Data analysis

Data entered into SPSS/PC and simple frequencies analysed.

Key findings

- Ethnicity was recorded for 100% of clients.
- 88.9% were classed as White and 11.1% as an ethnic minority. This was very similar to the breakdown from the previous audit (White = 88.7%, ethnic minority = 11.3%).
- The ethnic minority breakdown was:
  - Black Caribbean   20.6%
  - Black African   13.2%
  - Black Other   1.5%
  - Indian   29.4%
  - Pakistani   7.4%
  - Bangladeshi   0.0%
  - Chinese   0.0%
  - Other   27.9%

Feedback

Results of the audit were fed back to the team at the fortnightly Clinical Audit Meeting, and published in the annual Pathfinder Clinical Audit Report. The results were also presented to the Health Authority Steering Group in the CAT referrals (White = 88.88.9%; ethnic minority = 11.1%).

ORGANISATIONAL/MANAGEMENT PROCESSES

Change	In view of the relatively high representation of ethnic minorities in clients seen by CAT compared with the general population we do not plan to take any specific action except to continue to monitor ethnicity in line with Pathfinder policy.
Resources used	Staff time: CPN 50 hours, Administrative Assistant 20 hours.
Contact	Dr Colin Drummond, Reader in Addiction Psychiatry, St George's Hospital Medical School, Department of Addictive Behaviour & Psychological Medicine, Hunter Wing, Cranmer Terrace, London, SW17 0RE. Tel: 0181 682 6931; fax: 0181 682 6937; email: colin.drummond@sghms.ac.uk

ORGANISATIONAL/MANAGEMENT PROCESSES

Keyworker documentation re-audit

Aims	• To improve keyworker documentation.
	• To monitor patients more closely.
	• To increase clinical effectiveness.
	• To raise awareness within the staff about the importance of documentation.
	• To improve clinical and organisational processes and health outcomes.

Standards

1 80% of clients must be seen 5 times per quarter.
2 80% of notes must be up-to-date. As clients are seen fortnightly, there must be notations within the last 3 weeks.
3 There must be at least 5 notations per quarter (GP shared care 3 notations) for 70% of clients.
4 Workers must enquire on 70% of clients' mental health at least twice per quarter.
5 Workers must enquire on 70% of clients' general health at least once per quarter.
6 Workers must discuss HIV/hepatitis C/sexual health with 70% of clients at least once every 6 months.
7 Workers must discuss harm minimisation (safer IV use, safer sex) with 70% of clients at least once per quarter.
8 Where relevant, 70% of clients must have a urine sample taken once per quarter.
9 80% of clients should be seen by the doctor for a full medical assessment every 6 months.
10 Consent to liaise with GP must have been agreed or renewed within the last year for 70% of clients.
11 There must be at least 1 contact with 70% of clients' GPs every 6 months.
12 Workers must check whether clients are using on top at least once a quarter, for at least 70% of clients.
13 There must be at least 1 entry per quarter, in 70% of notes, to indicate that sites have been checked by the worker.
14 70% of those who are groin injectors or on amps must be checked by the doctor on at least one occasion per quarter.
15 100% of prescription records must be up-to-date.
16 Workers must assess whether clients have housing, benefit or legal problems at least once every 6 months, for 70% of clients.
17 Workers must have discussed short-term goals with 70% of clients at least once per quarter.

Evidence	Local consensus.
Staff involved	All drug service staff and the clinical audit department.
Sample	229 clients, representing a snapshot of the client population.
Data collection	By staff/keyworkers.
Data analysis	By clinical audit department.
Key findings	None – in progress.

Feedback	To drug service staff.
Re-audit	12 months.
Resources used	1 day for all staff and more time from the clinical audit department.
Notes	It was a problem changing some of the standards after the first audit and then not being able to compare year on year data very readily. If repeating this project we would do so on a smaller scale – we took on too much.
Contact	Sally Spurrell, Royal Free Drug Services, 457 Finchley Road, West Hampstead, London NW3 6HN. Tel: 0171 431 1731; fax: 0171 431 0860.

ORGANISATIONAL/MANAGEMENT PROCESSES

Clinical audit in substance misuse services

Methadone-related deaths

Background A high prevalence of drug-related deaths and a steep rise in methadone prescribing. A confidential medical enquiry into methadone-related deaths has been established to identify problems with and to improve clinical care and organisation of medical services.

Aim To improve clinical and organisational processes, health outcomes and user/carer satisfaction.

Standards

1 Before any enquiry, the coordinator is informed by the Procurator Fiscal that a drug-related death has occurred and either that forensic toxicology has revealed the presence of methadone or it is believed that the deceased was receiving prescribed methadone:
2 The coordinator must ask any doctor who is thought to have seen the patient in the 14 days prior to death to complete a standard questionnaire. All professional and patient identifiers are removed before this document is assessed.
3 The assessments must be carried out by 2 doctors, each acting independently. One of these is a GP with considerable experience of prescribing methadone to drug misusers and the other is a consultant psychiatrist with an interest in substance misuse.
4 The results of the assessments must be passed to the doctors who provided the original information. The doctors who feedback the assessments must not know the identities of the assessors in an individual case. All enquiry documents must be stored in a safe and any computerised data must be encrypted.
5 If the service has been involved in the care of a patient who is notified to the enquiry, the results of the assessments must be relayed to the doctor who provided the original information by a GP selected by the coordinator from the list mentioned in Standard 3. The identities of the assessors must be concealed as in Standard 4.
6 All doctors who receive an assessment of their care must complete a questionnaire on the personal and professional impact of the enquiry.
7 Reports must be produced assessing the main causes of methadone-related deaths, identifying any avoidable or substandard factors, suggesting possible improvements in care and bringing these findings to the attention of all relevant health care professionals. All forms and related documents must be destroyed after the preparation of these reports and before their publication.

Staff involved Prescribing doctors, GPs, psychiatrists, drug service doctors and coordinator.

Sample 34 deaths.

Data collection Standard written questionnaire.

Key findings
- In 2 cases, despite repeated efforts by enquiry staff, no further information could be obtained about any medical care that might have been given in the 14 days before death.
- Possible failings in clinical care were identified by the assessors in 18 cases and possible inadequate organisation of medical services in 22.

ORGANISATIONAL/MANAGEMENT PROCESSES

In 16 cases, shortcomings in both areas were thought possible. In several instances, the assessors commented that access to the case notes might have allowed a more comprehensive assessment to be performed.

- The primary causes of death given by the pathologists who performed the autopsies can be summarised as drug-related (25), infection (4), external trauma (2) or internal haemorrhage (1). 3 of the deaths appeared to be suicidal and the remainder were thought to be accidental.

- 24 patients had attended a doctor at some time during the 2-week period before death. 19 cases were receiving methadone on prescription. In 10 of these, methadone was thought by the pathologist to have contributed to the fatal outcome. In the remaining 13 cases, methadone was not being prescribed, though possibly contributed to 11 of the deaths.

- There were 3 deaths where methadone was the only drug identified at autopsy and in 2 of these it was judged to have contributed to the death. Benzodiazepines were detected in 19 cases, alcohol in 15 and chloral hydrate in 6. 2 patients were receiving antipsychotic medication for chronic schizophrenia.

- The mean dose of prescribed methadone was 46 mg (range 10–100). The mean duration of the prescription was 25 months (range 1 day to 70 months). In 14 of the 19 cases where methadone had been prescribed, the drug was being consumed under the supervision of a community pharmacist. In the 5 other cases, up to 28 days supply was being dispensed without supervision. There were 2 deaths that occurred within 14 days of commencing a prescription for methadone and in 1 of these cases methadone caused the death. All those being prescribed methadone were receiving the drug in the form of the oral mixture. No deaths following the use of injectable methadone or tablets of methadone were notified.

- In 13 cases no urinalysis for drugs of abuse had been carried out before a prescription for methadone was issued. All the deaths occurred in persons who were known to misuse drugs.

- 24 deaths occurred in the community, 23 in a domestic setting and 1 in a public place. In 5 cases, death was pronounced in an accident and emergency (A&E) department, usually after the patient had been brought in to hospital without any signs of life, while 3 cases were hospital in-patients. No deaths in police custody, prison or residential rehabilitation units were notified to the enquiry. 5 deaths took place within 14 days of discharge from prison. 1 person was being prescribed methadone from outside Glasgow and is thought to have been visiting the city at the time of death.

- 33 questionnaires on the impact of the enquiry were completed by the original informants. 28 stated that they had found cooperating with the enquiry to be helpful, both professionally and personally. 4 doctors did not answer this question, while 1 doctor questioned the validity of the process of the enquiry together with the impartiality of the assessors. No respondents reported finding the enquiry to be either professionally or personally harmful.

- 14 doctors stated that, in light of the enquiry findings, their prescribing practices for drug misusers would change. 1 doctor reported that drug misusers were no longer treated in their practice, 4 felt that the assessors' comments did not apply to them, 3 were unsure if their future practice would alter and 7 doctors thought it unlikely that it would. The remaining 4 questionnaires from A&E doctors did not show any indication for changing departmental resuscitation protocols.

Feedback	To original informants.
Change	<ul><li>All doctors caring for drug misuers should ensure that accurate doctor-to-doctor communication is established when patients move between services. Relying upon a history from the patient may be insufficient to allow proper care.</li><li>To reduce the illicit diversion of methadone, every opportunity must be taken to secure good compliance with the prescription. A community pharmacist supervising the self-administration of methadone is probably at present the best way of ensuring this.</li><li>Patients receiving methadone should be examined regularly for evidence of continued illicit drug use. This should consist of a physical examination for signs of recent injecting and urinalysis for drugs of abuse.</li><li>Greater Glasgow Health Board should examine ways of increasing the number of community pharmacies that open 7 days per week and that supervise methadone self-administration.</li><li>Doctors should recognise that any interruption in treatment may result in lost tolerance to opiates and that any resumption of prescribing may require a lower initial dose than was taken previously.</li><li>The compulsory detoxification from methadone treatment, which at present is the usual experience in prison, may increase the risk of death from an accidental opiate overdose soon after liberation. The Scottish Prison Service should continue to develop ways of prescribing methadone to patients whose treatment is interrupted by imprisonment.</li><li>Prescribers should ensure that pharmacists who dispense methadone are given sufficient information to allow the identity of a patient to be confirmed.</li><li>The further development of the enquiry should examine the possibility of obtaining the patients' case notes.</li></ul>
Re-audit	Hope to make it continuous.
Resources used	£100 postage and coordinator for 2 days a week.
Notes	Remarkably few problems. If repeating this audit, anonymised case records would be made available. *Advice:* Go for it but be prepared for a lot of work.
Contact	Dr Robert Scott, Glasgow Drug Problem Service, Woodside Health Centre, Barr Street, Glasgow, G20 7LR. Tel: 0141 531 9254; email: 113251.603@Compuserve.com

ORGANISATIONAL/MANAGEMENT PROCESSES

Referral of new patients with alcohol abuse problems

Background	The Home Detox Service in Ayrshire was established in 1995. The team delivers a 7-day locally accessible community-based alcohol and drug detoxification service to residents of Ayrshire and Arran. The service provides assessment, treatment and support to individuals who are withdrawing from problematic substance use.
Aim	To audit standards relating to initial contact and assessment times. When referred, patients should be contacted within 24 hours and assessed within 48 hours.
Standards	1 The source of the referral must be recorded. 2 The mode of referral must be recorded. 3 The patient must be contacted within 24 hours. 4 The patient must be assessed within 48 hours.
Staff involved	Charge Nurse, Research Assistant.
Sample	Randomly selected cases referred to the Home Detox Team over a 6-month period ($n=50$).
Data collection	Patient case notes were checked for referral source, mode of referral, initial contact and assessment times.
Data analysis	Descriptive statistics were used to analyse the data.
Key findings	• 100% of referral sources were recorded. 92% were referred by a GP, 4% by a hospital, 2% by psychiatric services and 2% by 'other'. • 100% of referral modes were recorded. 84% were made by telephone, 14% by letter and 2% by fax. • 80% of patients were contacted within 24 hours. • 58% of patients were assessed within 48 hours.
Contact	Angela Kerr, Research Assistant, Home Detox Team, Addiction Services, Dundonald Health Centre, 2 Newfield Drive, Kilmarnock, KA2 9EW. Tel: 01563 851338; fax: 01563 850684; email: IRT@addun.demon.co.uk

ORGANISATIONAL/MANAGEMENT PROCESSES

Secondary benzodiazepine use among heroin addicts attending a drug dependency unit

Background	Recording and management of secondary benzodiazepine use among heroin addicts was thought to be poor.
Aims	• To improve recording accuracy and hence clinical care. • To improve clinical and organisational processes and health outcomes.
Standards	1 Every file must include accurate recording of usage. 2 Inappropriate use must be noted.
Evidence	British National Formulary dose ranges.
Staff involved	Clinical psychologist and audit assistant.
Sample	Approximately 200 service users.
Data collection	Manual search of clinical records.
Key findings	• Recording was inconsistent and incomplete. Only 17 could be confidently described as accurately recorded. • 85 cases were classified as inappropriate use (regular or intermittent).
Feedback	Verbal and written feedback was given to the whole team.
Change	• All drug use to be regularly recorded – type, route and quantity. • Client self-reports should be regularly matched against urine drug screen report. • Protocol for benzodiazepine prescribing management devised.
Re-audit	5 years.
Resoures used	60 hours, researcher time and phone calls to GPs for verification.
Notes	Problems encountered included inconsistent standards of recording and the need to check prescribing records with GPs. The variability of service users' habits (and their GPs) can make accurate recording difficult. *Advice*: involve team members more to generate ownership of data. Be prepared for a worrying report.
Contact	Dr Daphne Rumball, The Bure Centre, 7 Unthank Road, Norwich, NR2 2PA. Tel: 01603 667955; fax: 01603 762701; email: Bure@globalnet.co.uk

ORGANISATIONAL/ MANAGEMENT PROCESSES

Client satisfaction with service

Aims	• To improve clinical processes, health outcomes and service user/carer satisfaction. • To highlight the area of project deficit
Standards	1 All agencies must survey client group regarding satisfaction with their service at least every 2 years. 2 All clients seen in a 1-month period must be asked to express their level of satisfaction with the service using questionnaires or other suitable methods. 3 The number of clients seen in the time period and the size of the sample questioned must be recorded. 4 There must a procedure set up for informing clients of the results obtained. 5 There must be a procedure for feeding results back into a service planning process. 6 There must be a procedure for involving clients in the design of the next survey. 7 A date must be fixed for the next survey, within 2 years of the last.
Evidence	Audit project team discussed formulation of standards.
Staff involved	All Community Drug Service staff and peer auditors.
Sample	All clients over a 1-month period.
Data collection	Specially designed questionnaire.
Key findings	In progress.
Re-audit	Within 2 years.
Contact	Dr Barry Blackstone, Community Drugs Service, Danerel House, Danerel Close, Off Malden Road, Devonport, Plymouth, PL1 4JX. Tel: 01752 566670; fax: 01752 566676.

Client satisfaction with the substance misuse detoxification programme

Aims
- To obtain opinions from users of the service to ensure improved delivery of care.
- To promote awareness of addiction.
- To ensure that high standards are maintained through staff awareness of service provision, ensuring continual growth and expansion of the service.
- To enable users and referring agencies to become more aware of the benefits and advantages of the service.
- To identify staff training needs.
- To identify the benefits/disadvantages of the programme and the philosophy of care.

Standards
1. All clients must be assessed for admission within 7 days.
2. All clients must be admitted within 7 days.
3. All clients must be satisfied with the answers that they are given to their questions.
4. All clients must be satisfied with the explanation of their treatment.
5. All clients must be satisfied that they were given an explanation of the contract, house rules, visiting policy and other policies.
6. Policies relating to property searching/urine testing must be explained to clients' satisfaction.
7. All clients must be introduced to other clients/staff on duty on admission.
8. All clients must be shown around the unit on admission.
9. All clients must be made aware of fire procedure, either in written or verbal form.
10. All clients must receive an information booklet.
11. All clients must be satisfied with the information booklet.
12. All clients must be made aware of who their named nurse or keyworker is.
13. All clients must be made aware of who their named nurse or keyworker was on the day of admission.
14. All clients must meet their named nurse/keyworker.
15. All clients must meet their named nurse/keyworker within 3 days of admission.
16. The care plan and process must be explained to the satisfaction of the client.
17. All clients must be involved in care planning.
18. All clients must agree to the care plan.
19. All clients must sign the care plan.
20. Care plans must be evaluated on the appropriate date.
21. All clients must be involved in the evaluation of the care plan.
22. All clients' feelings must be noted.
23. All clients must be offered one-to-one sessions with their keyworker.
24. All clients must be satisfied with their keyworker's performance during their stay.
25. All clients must be satisfied with the explanation of their particular detox programme.

26 All clients must be satisfied with the explanation of the use and side-effects of their medication.
27 All clients must be satisfied with their general physical comfort during detox.
28 All clients must be satisfied with the speed of detox.
29 All clients must be satisfied with the attitude of nursing staff towards them.
30 All clients must feel that their withdrawals were adequately controlled.
31 All clients must be regularly clinically assessed for withdrawals.
32 All clients must feel able to approach staff to discuss withdrawals/medication.
33 All clients must be satisfied with the content of the unit programme.
34 All clients must be satisfied with the number of groups/activities per day.
35 All clients must be satisfied with the punctuality of groups.
36 All clients must be satisfied with the content of groups.
37 All clients must be satisfied with the attitude of staff.
38 All clients must feel that the groups were appropriate to them.
39 All clients must feel that they learned/gained something from their participation in a group.
40 All clients and their relatives must feel that they gained something from Family Support, if it was used.
41 All clients must be able to go to church on Sundays if they want.
42 If it is not possible to go to church on Sundays, the client must be given an explanation why.
43 All clients must be satisfied with the input and attitude of nursing staff.
44 All clients must be satisfied with the input and attitude of their consultant.
45 All clients must be satisfied with the input and attitude of doctors.
46 All clients must be satisfied with the input and attitude of nursing staff.
47 All clients must be satisfied with the input and attitude of project staff.
48 All clients must be satisfied with the input and attitude of any other staff.
49 All clients must feel involved in discharge planning and arranging follow-up care.
50 All clients going on to rehab must be satisfied with any help they need choosing a rehab.
51 For clients going on to rehab, assessment for rehab must take less than 7 days.
52 For clients going on to rehab, assessment for finance must take less than 7 days.
53 For clients going on to rehab, all clients must be satisfied with the way assessments are carried out.
54 All clients who see a doctor must be satisfied with the time it took for the doctor to see them.
55 All clients who see a doctor must be satisfied with the attitude of the doctor.
56 All clients who see a doctor must be satisfied with the explanation of any treatment prescribed.

Evidence	Local protocols.
Staff involved	Unit Manager, clinical audit department and nursing staff.

Clinical audit in substance misuse services

Sample		All clients who attended over a 6-month period ($n=123$; number of questionnaires returned = 58).	
Data collection		A questionnaire was devised and given to clients.	
Data analysis		Descriptive statistics.	
Key findings		Compliance with standards was as follows:	
	1	73%	29	74%
	2	64%	30	96%
	3	82%	31	87%
	4	82%	32	92%
	5	82%	33	75%
	6	93%	34	62%
	7	95%	35	43%
	8	90%	36	68%
	9	83%	37	75%
	10	88%	38	96%
	11	74%	39	96%
	12	93%	40	100%
	13	59%	41	80%
	14	96%	42	89%
	15	94%	43	71%
	16	88%	44	73%
	17	83%	45	75%
	18	93%	46	74%
	19	87%	47	66%
	20	74%	48	61%
	21	82%	49	86%
	22	82%	50	100%
	23	80%	51	56%
	24	85%	52	81%
	25	71%	53	84%
	26	68%	54	67%
	27	68%	55	67%
	28	72%	56	67%

Feedback	Unit Manager fedback to all Unit staff.

Change

- Keyworkers must ensure that clients knows their name and should follow this up 2 days after admission.
- Staff must ensure that clients are given the information booklet on admission.
- Clients must be asked what specific information they would like to be included in the Information Booklet.
- The fire procedure must be included in the admission procedure.
- Staff must encourage the client to ask questions about the care plan to ensure their understanding in the process.
- Staff must receive more training in the care plan process.
- Care plans must be audited to ascertain whether they have been signed, re-evaluated and resigned in the past. Also set up monitoring system to ensure that this is always done in the future.
- Remind staff of the value of one-to-one sessions.
- The keyworker must work with the client to ensure the satisfactory explanation of the detox programme.

USER SATISFACTION AND OUTCOMES

- The content of the programme must be regularly discussed with the clients to obtain feedback.
- Staff must consider how to provide longer and more varied leisure time and activities for service users.

Re-audit   No plans.

Contact   John Wilkins, Clinical Audit Manager, Thames Gateway NHS Trust, St Bartholomew's, New Road, Rochester, Kent, ME1 1DS. Tel: 01634 810900; fax: 01634 810948.

Outcomes of drug detoxification clinic

Background	The in-patient service believed that it had a poor success rate.
Aim	To increase the success rate of both out-patient and in-patient opiate detoxification.
Standards	1 15% of out-patient clients must successfully complete detoxification. 2 70% of in-patient clients must successfully complete detoxification.
Evidence	DoH targets.
Staff involved	External auditor.
Sample	197 clients discharged during a 6-month period.
Data collection	From case notes.
Data analysis	Descriptive statistics.
Key findings	• 7.9% of out-patient clients were successfully detoxified. • 66.6% of in-patient clients were successfully detoxified.
Feedback	Results discussed as a hospital audit meeting.
Change	Try to improve the success rate of our out-patient detoxification service.
Re-audit	Not planned.
Resources used	External auditor time only.
Contact	Dr Andrew D. T. Robinson, Consultant Psychiatrist, Grampian Healthcare NHS Trust, Substance Misuse Service, Fulton Clinic, Royal Cornhill Hospital, Aberdeen. Tel: 01224 663131; fax: 01224 404975.

USER SATISFACTION AND OUTCOMES

Patient satisfaction and outcomes in a community alcohol service

Background

1997 was a year of change in the service and it was therefore considered an opportune time to test the quality of the service provided against the opinion of the service users.

Aims

- To measure effectiveness of the service generally and relate these results to individual client progress criteria.
- To clarify strengths and weaknesses with a view to utilising limited resources as efficiently as possible in the future.
- To give service users a say in service development.
- To find out if a client's journey through treatment helps them specifically with alcohol problems.
- To compare results with local standards.

Standards

Services

1 All clients must find the opening hours of the service satisfactory.
2 All clients must find the waiting area to be satisfactory.
3 All clients must find the staff friendly and approachable.
4 All clients must be given time to ask questions during their plan of care.
5 All clients must be kept up to date with their plan of care.
6 All staff must introduce themselves to clients during the client's first attendance.
7 All staff must ask clients how they would like to be addressed.
8 All clients must be informed of what to do if they have any worries.
9 All clients must find the explanation of their treatment by their counsellor satisfactory.
10 The treatment programme must meet all the clients' needs.
11 All clients must be sufficiently satisfied to recommend the service to a friend in need of similar help.
12 All clients must be satisfied with the amount of help they received from their counsellor.
13 The services received must help clients deal with their problems.
14 All clients must be sufficiently satisfied to be willing to return if you were asked to seek help.

Individual outcomes

15 Clients' use of alcohol must decrease.
16 Clients' use of prescribed drugs must decrease.
17 Clients' physical health must improve.
18 Clients' psychological health must improve.
19 Clients' accommodation status must improve.
20 Clients' employment status must improve.
21 Clients' relationships with relatives must improve.
22 Clients' relationships with partners must improve.
23 Clients' criminal activity must decrease.
24 Clients' attendance records must improve.

Staff involved	Nursing staff, clinical audit department.
Sample	30 clients attending the Community Alcohol Service.
Data collection	By questionnaire distributed to clients and return in pre-paid envelopes.
Data analysis	Qualitative and quantitative data analysed.

Key findings	
	Services
	1 96% of clients found the opening hours of the service satisfactory.
	2 80% of clients found the waiting area to be satisfactory.
	3 100% of clients found the staff friendly and approachable.
	4 100% of clients were given time to ask questions during their plan of care.
	5 93% of clients were be kept up-to-date with their plan of care.
	6 100% of staff introduced themselves to clients during the client's first attendance.
	7 77% of clients were asked how they would like to be addressed.
	8 90% of clients were informed of what to do if they have any worries.
	9 96% of clients found the explanation of their treatment by their counsellor satisfactory.
	10 The treatment programme met almost all the needs for 50% of clients and most of the needs of 50% of clients.
	11 100% of clients were sufficiently satisfied to recommend the service to a friend in need of similar help.
	12 96% of clients were satisfied with the amount of help they received from their counsellor.
	13 The services received helped 100% of clients deal with their problems.
	14 100% of clients were sufficiently satisfied to be willing to return if they were asked to seek help.
	Individual outcomes
	15 Clients' use of alcohol decreased in 57% of cases, ceased in 3% and stabilised in 20%. Alcohol was not used in 20% of cases.
	16 Clients' use of prescribed drugs decreased in 10% of cases, stabilised in 17% and increased in 17%. Prescribed drugs were not used in 50%.
	17 Clients' physical health improved in 67% of cases, stabilised in 10% and became worse in 17%.
	18 Clients' psychological health improved in 67% of cases, stabilised in 30% and became worse in 3%.
	19 Clients' accommodation status improved in 17% and remained unchanged in 83%.
	20 Clients' employment status improved in 3% of cases, remained unchanged in 80% of cases and became worse in 3%.
	21 Clients' relationships with relatives improved in 37% of cases, remained unchanged in 47% and became worse in 7%.
	22 Clients' relationships with partners improved in 33% of cases, remained unchanged in 40% and became worse in 10%.
	23 Clients' criminal activity ceased in 3% of cases, remained unchanged in 57% and increased in 3%.
	24 Clients' attendance records improved in 30% of cases and remained unchanged in 57%.

Feedback	Report distributed to managers/purchasers/colleagues and available to clients.

USER SATISFACTION AND OUTCOMES

Change	None.

Re-audit — Planning to re-audit but concentrating on refining outcomes.

Resources used — Staffing/admin support.

Contact — Steve Owen, Coordinator – West Lancashire Drug and Alcohol Services, North Sefton and West Lancashire NHS Trust, 75–77 Westgate, Skelmersdale, Lancashire, WN8 8LP. Tel: 01695 50740; fax: 01695 51620.

Patient satisfaction and outcomes in a community drugs team

Background
: The previous audit of patient satisfaction and outcomes in a community alcohol team was also undertaken in a community drugs team. The aims and standards were the same.

Staff involved
: Nursing staff and clinical audit department.

Sample
: 15 clients attending the Community Drug Team.

Data collection
: By questionnaire distributed to clients and returned in a box located in the waiting area. The outcomes questionnaire was distributed separately from the satisfaction questionnaire.

Data analysis
: Qualitative and quantitative data analysed.

Key findings

Services
1. 100% of clients found the opening hours of the service satisfactory.
2. 87% of clients found the waiting area to be satisfactory.
3. 100% of clients found the staff friendly and approachable.
4. 100% of clients were given time to ask questions during their plan of care.
5. 93% of clients were be kept up to date with their plan of care.
6. 93% of staff introduced themselves to clients during the client's first attendance.
7. 87% of clients were asked how they would like to be addressed and 13% didn't know whether or not they had been asked.
8. 100% of clients were informed of what to do if they had any worries.
9. 100% of clients found the explanation of their treatment by their counsellor satisfactory.
10. The treatment programme met almost all the needs for 40% of clients, most of the needs of 50% of clients and few of the needs of 20%.
11. 100% of clients were sufficiently satisfied to recommend the service to a friend in need of similar help.
12. 100% of clients were satisfied with the amount of help they received from their counsellor.
13. The services received helped 100% of clients deal with their problems.
14. 100% of clients were sufficiently satisfied to be willing to return if they were asked to seek help.

Individual outcomes
15. Clients' use of alcohol decreased in 33% of cases, stabilised in 20% and increased in 10%.
16. Clients' use of prescribed drugs decreased in 37% of cases, stabilised in 33% and increased in 27%.
17. Clients' physical health improved in 53% of cases, stabilised in 27% and became worse in 17%.

18 Clients' psychological health improved in 27% of cases, stabilised in 50% and became worse in 23% .

19 Clients' accommodation status improved in 13%, remained unchanged in 70% and became worse in 17%.

20 Clients' employment status improved in 13% of cases, remained unchanged in 70% of cases and became worse in 17%.

21 Clients' relationships with relatives improved in 53% of cases, remained unchanged in 27% and became worse in 17%.

22 Clients' relationships with partners improved in 33% of cases, remained unchanged in 37% and became worse in 27% .

23 Clients' criminal activity decreased in 60% of cases, remained unchanged in 27% and increased in 13%.

24 Clients' attendance records improved in 37% of cases and remained unchanged in 63%.

Feedback	Report distributed to managers/purchasers/colleagues and available to clients.
Change	None.
Re-audit	A larger sample size would be needed. A further audit into outcomes for the individual client is necessary.
Resources used	Staffing/admin support.
Contact	Steve Owen, Coordinator – West Lancashire Drug and Alcohol Services, West Lancashire Health Services, 75–77 Westgate, Skelmersdale, Lancashire, WN8 8LP. Tel: 01695 50740; fax: 01695 51620.

User satisfaction with methadone treatment

Background   Substance misuse services at Newtown Hospital in Worcester were started in 1996. We have 120 registered users. It was felt that there was a need to evaluate service to ascertain its performance in relation to the level of satisfaction among its users.

Aim   To improve organisational processes and service user satisfaction.

Standards
1   Users must be satisfied with the comfort and attractiveness of the facility.
2   The receptionists and secretaries must be friendly and make users feel comfortable.
3   The service received by users must be appropriate.
4   The person each user worked most closely with must be competent and knowledgeable.
5   Users must be satisfied with the quality of the service they received.
6   Users must be satisfied with the amount of help they received.
7   The services received must have helped users to deal more effectively with their problem.
8   Users must be satisfied with the service they received overall.
9   On their initial visit, users must be seen promptly.
10 Users must be willing to recommend the programme to friends or family if they were in need of similar help.

Evidence   Local consensus.

Sample   72 patients.

Data collection   Data collected by clinical staff on a self-completion multi-dimensional structured format.

Data analysis   Descriptive statistics.

Key findings
1   73% of users the comfort and attractiveness of the facility 'excellent' or 'good'.
2   94% of users found the receptionists and secretaries were friendly and made them feel comfortable.
3   36% of users felt that almost all of their needs had been met; 42% felt that most of their needs had been met; 19% felt that only a few of their needs had been met; and 3% felt that none of their needs were met.
4   49% of users felt that the person they worked most closely with was very competent and 39% felt that the person competent.
5   83% of users were satisfied with the quality of the service they received.
6   75% of users were satisfied with the amount of help they received.
7   84% of users felt that the services received helped them to deal more effectively with their problem.
8   86% of users were satisfied with the service they received overall.
9   On their initial visit, 81% of users must be seen promptly.
10 78% of users were willing to recommend the programme to friends or family if they were in need of similar help.
The overall rating was: excellent – 33%; good – 48%; fair – 12%; poor – 7%.

Change	No change was noted.
Re-audit	Not planned.
Contact	Dr Ruth White, Consultant Psychiatrist, Worcestershire Community Healthcare and Mental Health NHS Trust, Mental Health Directorate, Newtown Hospital, Newtown Road, Worcester, WR5 1JG. Tel: 01905 763333; fax: 01905 351231.

References and further reading

ASSOCIATION OF COMMUNITY HEALTH COUNCILS FOR ENGLAND AND WALES (1997) *Hungry in Hospital*. London: ACHEW.

COLLEGE OF OCCUPATIONAL THERAPISTS (1998) *Clinical Audit Information Pack*. London: College of Occupational Therapists.

BALOGH, R., BOND, S., DUNN, J., ET AL (199) *Newcastle Clinical Audit Toolkit for Mental Health*. Newcastle: Centre for Health Services Research, University of Newcastle upon Tyne.

BUTTERY, Y. (1994) *The Development of Audit. Findings of a National Survey of Healthcare Provider Units in England*. London: CASPE Research.

CRAG WORKING GROUP ON MENTAL ILLNESS (1994) *The Management of Alcohol Withdrawal and Delirium Tremens*. Lothian: CRAG.

DENNIS, N. (1995) Consumer audit in the NHS. *British Journal of Hospital Medicine*, **53**, 532–534.

DEPARTMENT OF HEALTH (1989) *Working for Patients*. White Paper. London: DoH.

—— (1990) *Medical Audit*. Working Paper. London: DoH.

—— (1994) *Clinical Audit in the Nursing and Therapy Professions*. London: DoH.

—— (1994) *Improving Care Through Clinical Audit: Proceedings of a One-Day Conference on Clinical Audit for the Health Care Professions*. London: DoH.

—— (1994) *Medical Audit in Primary Care: A Collation of Evaluation Projects 1991–1993*. London: DoH.

—— (1996) *Immunisation Against Infectious Disease*. London: HMSO.

—— (1996) *Clinical Audit in the NHS*. London: DoH.

—— (1997) *The New NHS: Modern, Dependable*. White Paper. London: DoH.

—— (1999) *Statistical Bulletin*. London: DoH.

DIXON, N. (1996) Good practice in clinical audit – a summary of selected literature to support criteria for clinical audit. In *NCCA Clinical Audit Action Pack. A Practical Approach*. London: National Centre for Clinical Audit.

EXWORTHY, M., STEINER, A. & BARNARD, S. (1996) The future of clinical audit: the outcomes of a consensus conference. *Journal of Clinical Effectiveness*, 1, 129–133.

FIRTH-COZENS, J. (1993) *Audit in Mental Health Services*. Hove: Lawrence Earlbaum.

GAILEY, F. (1996) *Clinical Audit Enabler: A Clinical Audit Resource Reference Guide*. Edinburgh: Lothian Clinical Audit.

LELLIOTT, P. (1994) Clinical audit in psychiatry. *Hospital Update*, February, 82–91.

—— & AUDINI, B. (1996) *An Audit Pack for Monitoring the Care Programme Approach*. London: NHS Executive.

LORD, J. & LITTLEJOHNS, P. (1997) Evaluating healthcare policies: the case of clinical audit. *British Medical Journal*, **315**, 668–671.

LUGON, M. & SECKER-WALKER, J. (1999) *Clinical Governance. Making it Happen*. London: Royal Society of Medicine Press.

MELTZER, H., GILL, B. & PETTICREW, M. (1995) *The Prevalence of Psychiatric Morbidity Among Adults Aged 16–64 Living in Private Households in Great Britain*. London: OPCS Publications Unit.

MORRELL, C. & HARVEY, G. (1999) *The Clinical Audit Handbook. Improving the Quality of Care*. London: Harcourt-Brace.

OFFICE OF POPULATION, CENSUS & SURVEYS (1996) *Living in Britain: Results from th 1994 General Household Survey*. London: HMSO.

PRIMARY HEALTH CARE CLINICAL AUDIT WORKING GROUP OF CLINICAL OUTCOMES GROUP AND CLINICAL OUTCOMES GROUP (1994) *Clinical Audit in Primary Care*, pp. 1–62. London: DoH.

RIORDAN, J. & MOCKLER, D. (1997) *Clinical Audit in Mental Health. Towards a Multidisciplinary Approach*. Chichester: John Wiley & Sons.

ROYAL COLLEGE OF PSYCHAITRISTS (1994) *The General Hospital Management of Adult Deliberate Self-Harm*. London: Royal College of Psychiatrists.

SCOTTISH DRUGS FORUM ALL-PARTY POLICY WORKING GROUP (1999) *Drug Use in Scotland – A Shared Agenda for the Scottish Parliament*. Glasgow: Scottish Drugs Forum.

THOMPSON, D. (1993) *Learning Disabilities: The Fundamental Facts*. London: Mental Health Foundation.

WALSHE, K. (1995) *Evaluating Clinical Audit: Past Lessons, Future Directions*. London: Royal Society of Medicine Press.

—— & BENNETT, J. (1991) *Guidelines on Medical Audit and Confidentiality*. Brighton: Brighton Health Authority/South East Thames Regional Health Authority.

—— & COLES, J. (1993) *Evaluating Audit. Developing a Framework*. London: CASPE Research.

Clinical audit in substance misuse services

Resources

Alcoholics Anonymous
PO Box 1
Stonebow House
Stonebow
York
YO1 2NJ
Tel (London): 020 7352 3001
Tel (York): 01904 644026

Alcoholics Anonymous
109 South Circular Road
Leonard's Corner
Dublin
Ireland
Tel: 00 353(1) 453 8998

Centre for Evidence-Based Mental Health
Department of Psychiatry
University of Oxford
Warneford Hospital
Oxford OX3 7JX
Tel: 01865 226 476
Fax: 01865 793 101
Website: cembh.enquiries@psychiatry.ox.ac.uk

Clinical Audit Association
Room 46, Cleethorpes Centre
Jackson Place
Wilton Road
Humberston
South Humberside
DN36 4AS
Tel: 01472 210682
Website: www.the-caa-ltd.demon.co.uk

The Clinical Governance Resource and Development Unit
Department of General Practice and Primary
Healthcare
University of Leicester
Leicester General Hospital
Gwendolen Road
Leicester LE5 4PW
Tel: 0116 258 4873
Fax: 0116 258 4982
Email: cgrdu@le.ac.uk
Website: www.le.ac.uk/cgrdu

Clinical Resource and Audit Group (CRAG)
Room 205, St Andrew's House
Regent Road
Edinburgh EH1 3DE
Tel: 0131 244 2235

College of Occupational Therapists
106–114 Borough High Street
London SE1 1LB
Tel: 0171 357 6480
Fax: 0171 450 229
Website: www.cot.co.uk/contact.html

College Research Unit
Royal College of Psychiatrists
11 Grosvenor Crescent
London SW1X 7EE
Tel: 0171 235 2351
Fax: 0171 235 2954
Email: CRULondon@compuserve.com
Website: www.rcpsych.ac.uk/cru/crufs/html.

The College Research Unit's activities include
coordinating national audits and producing
information sheets, guidelines bibliographies,
evidence-base briefings and clinical audit
publications.

Community Practitioners and Health Visitors Association (CPHVA) Clinical Audit Database
50 Southwark Street
London SE1 1UN
Tel: 0171 717 4086/7/8

Eli Lilly National Clinical Audit Centre
Department of General Practice and Primary
Health Care
University of Leicester
Leicester General Hospital
Gwendolen Road
Leicester LE5 4PW
Tel: 0116 258 4873
Fax: 0116 258 4982
Email: gpaudit@le.ac.uk
Website: www.le.ac.uk/clinaudit

King's Fund
11-13 Cavendish Square
London W1M 0AN
Tel: 0171 307 2400
Fax: 0171 307 2801
Website: www.KingsFund.co.uk

National Drugs Helpline
Tel: 0800 77 66 00

National Institute for Clinical Excellence
90 Long Acre
London WC2E 9RZ
Tel: 0171 849 3444
Fax: 0171 849 3127
Email: ncca@ncca.org.uk
Website: www.nice.org.uk

Pavilion Publishing
8 St George's Place
Brighton
East Sussex
BN1 4GB
Tel: 01273 623222
Fax: 01273 625526
Email: pavpub@pavilion.co.uk
Website: www.pavpub.com

Royal College of Nursing, Nursing and Midwifery Audit Information Service
20 Cavendish Square
London W1M 0AB
Tel: 0171 647 3831
Fax: 0171 647 3437

Royal College of Paediatrics and Child Health
50 Hallam Street
London W1N 6DE
Tel: 0171 307 5600
fax: 0171 307 5601
Email: enquiries@rcpch.ac.uk

Royal College of Speech and Language Therapists
7 Bath Place
Rivington Street
London EC2A 3SU
Tel: 0171 613 3855
Fax: 0171 613 3854

Scottish Audit Network
Tel: 01236 748748

Scottish Clinical Audit Resource Centre (SCARC)
University of Glasgow
1 Horselethill Road
Glasgow G12 9LX
Tel: 0141 330 6190
Fax: 0141 330 6912
Email: Sue.Kinn@udcf.gla.ac.uk
Website: gopher.gla.ac.uk/Acad/PGMedSCARC/open

Clinical audit in substance misuse services

Feedback form

We hope that you have found *Improving the Care of People in Substance Misuse Services: Clinical Audit Project Examples* useful and we would very much appreciate your feedback. Your comments will be incorporated, where possible, into future editions of this publication.

1 Have you found this book useful? ☐ Yes ☐ No
  If yes, please describe briefly how this book has been used in practice.

_____

_____

_____

_____

_____

2 Are there information sources that you think ought to have been included in this book? Please list full references where possible.

_____

_____

_____

_____

3 Do you have suggestions for topics areas in which you would like to see future clinical audit books developed?

_____

_____

_____

_____

4 Do you have any general suggestions about this book that would improve its usefulness?

_____

_____

_____

_____

5 What is your profession?

6 How many people in your organisation have access to this CAPE?

If you have any further comments, please feel free to attach extra paper.

Thank you for taking the time to complete this form. Your comments will be considered carefully.
Please photocopy and return to:
Kirsty MacLean Steel, Royal College of Psychiatrists' Research Unit, FREEPOST – LON602, 11 Grosvenor Crescent, London, SW1X 7YS. Fax: 0171 235 2954.

Project submission form

If you have any clinical audit projects you would like included in future editions of this book, please copy and complete this form and return it to:

Kirsty MacLean Steel
Royal College of Psychiatrists' Research Unit
11 Grosvenor Crescent
London SW1X 7EE

Name: _____

Address: _____

_____

Telephone: _____   **Fax:** _____

Email: _____

Clinician responsible for audit (if different from above): _____

Date of audit (year) and period of time over which data were collected:

_____

Notes about the completion of form: please continue on separate sheet if necessary and attach your audit report to refer to if this is easier. If you have any questions regarding the information requested on this form, please contact Kirsty MacLean Steel or Claire Palmer on 0171 235 2351, ext. 282.

Clinical audit project title	
Background Why was this audit considered important (i.e. why was this topic selected)?	
Aims and objectives Did the audit aim to improve (please tick more than one if appropriate):	(a) clinical processes (e.g. assessment, treatment) ☐ (b) organisational processes (e.g. waiting times, information recording) ☐ (c) health outcomes ☐ (d) service user or carer satisfaction with service ☐ (e) the use of resources ☐

Standards	Standard 1: _____
Did you set explicit, measurable standards against which practice could be compared? Please outline:	Standard 2: _____
	Standard 3: _____
	Standard 4: _____
	Standard 5: _____
On what were the standards based, e.g. local consensus, research evidence, national guidelines, feedback from service users etc.?	
Involvement Who was involved in the audit?	
Assessing practice against the standards What was the sample size and how was it selected? How were the data collected? How were the data analysed?	
Key findings	
Feedback of findings To whom were the results of the study communicated and how?	

Suggestions for change Following the audit have you come up with suggestions for changes in practice? If so, what are they? If not, why not?	
Changing practice Have there been any significant things which have either helped, or prevented, change from being implemented? Please describe.	
Re-audit After how long do you plan to re-audit?	
Resources Approximately how much staff time was taken to complete the audit cycle (hours)? Were any other costs or resources needed?	
Evaluating the audit What problems did you encounter (if any) in undertaking the audit? If you were doing this project again, are there any aspects of the audit you would change?	
What advice would you offer to someone attempting a similar audit?	